Happy Are We!

Published by Covenant Communications, Inc. American Fork, Utah

Printed in China
First Printing: September 2013

18 17 16 15 14 13   10 9 8 7 6 5 4 3 2 1

ISBN-13 978-1-62108-525-6

Happy Are We!

35 YEARS OF HUMOR FROM VAL CHADWICK BAGLEY

Are you going to be long?

Well, Elder, you certainly know how to break the ice.

No, I asked about your home teaching, *not* your home planet.

If the Elders Quorum was in charge of face painting...
Face Painting 25¢

And they call *us* a "peculiar people" . . .

It's not a punk haircut—I have early morning seminary.

Are we there yet? He's making faces at me! She's on my side! I feel cart-sick.

I got the popcorn off the apricot tree!

I can't remember if I'm putting them up or taking them down . . .

Sorry to cut your talk short, Brother Gabwell!

Who me? I'm with the Sweeny reunion, but the food is better over here.

Whoever said Sunday is a day of rest never taught Primary!
CTR

Okay, Elder, this isn't working.

You had the blueprints upside down!

You misunderstood. I said I'm a Mia Maid, not a mermaid.

Ha, ha, ha! That was a good one! But seriously, where is the outlet?

I know you're still learning the language, but you just told him that reading the Book of Mormon will give him mighty heartburn.

How could you forget my mother's birthday? It's right here on the calendar!

I've been asked to speak on the distractions of the worl— Hold on. I'm getting a text.

This must be my lucky day!
US MAIL

See, it says right here: the last shall be first and the first shall be last.

I think there may have been a misunderstanding
about your responsibilities as a Beehive advisor . . .

Aaahhh! Secret combination! Secret combination!

. . . and then King Noah made his getaway in the ark!

Okay, I get the rock, but I have no idea what paper and scissors are.

Don't think of it as a "Dear John." Think of yourself as a free agent!

Opposition in all things.

We'd like to call you to serve as a quilting specialist.

Hi, Honey. How was girls' camp?

All I said was I've never had green Jell-O with shredded carrots before.

Is it just me or do you always seem to do the grocery shopping on the Saturday before fast Sunday?

Well, yes. As a matter of fact they *are* engraved in stone.

Exodus 20:15—"Thou shalt not steal."

. . . but other than that you had a good time?

Sure I helped—I carried it in here.

I've been meaning to talk to you about your helmet, Elder Erickson . . .

Getting a technical foul isn't really the kind of thing you need to come and see me about.

Honey, have you seen my shield?

So, what do you think? I took breakfast, lunch, and dinner and combined them into one convenient drink.

We were out of cream of mushroom, cream of potato, and cream of broccoli, so I used cream of wheat.

I don't suppose you'd believe that a dog ate my homework?

Nobody likes a backseat driver, Elder.

My hair was released before I was.

Is licking the tithing envelope breaking my fast?

He followed us home. Can we keep him?

So, when I have my perfect, resurrected body, will I be able to pick up a "7–10 split"?

I couldn't find the remote for three days. Someone hid it under my scriptures.

Any questions? . . . And, no, Noah's wife's name was not Joan of Ark.

He wears them every time we sing "Jesus Wants Me for a Sunbeam."

Do you think it's too much for a first date?

But calling you an eight-cow woman was supposed to be a compliment.

Why do I need to learn math if we'll be creating worlds without number?

So, what do you know about the Mormon Church?

Are you sure that's the instrument you want to play, Moroni?

Oops, my mistake! It's an ad from John Deere, not a "Dear John."

No, I didn't say it was lucky to swallow a bug. I said it was lucky that I didn't.

We're doing what the song says: "Put Your Shoulder to the Wheel."

I just received a text from the bishop that says it's not appropriate to text during church . . .

I thought that because we're living in the last days I didn't need to clean my room.

Mom! It's the gnome teachers!

I have a book of remembrance. I just can't remember where . . .

Yes, it's a nice tractor, but we're tracting.

They cancelled Scouts—no one brought a basketball.

Are you sure you're on the right trek?

What part of "thou shalt not" don't you understand?

That is the worst case of jet lag I've ever seen.

I've got a bad feeling about this!
DINER
TODAY'S SPECIAL
ALL YOU CAN EAT!

You haven't eaten the casserole yet . . .

I know it's the last day of the month, but we started out on the *first!*

"There is sunshine in my soul today . . ."

Mom! Billy's been playing Ammon with my dolls again!

She feels like a failure because she came back from trek without a single blister.

We'd like to talk to you about the law of tithing.

Why do you guys always wait till the last day of the month to do your home teaching?

Do you know "*Silent* Night"?

Happens every time he tries to take inventory.

Sister Claus, we'd like to call you to serve in the nursery.

Yes, we're Santa's little helpers. No, we're not going to do your home teaching!

All right!
New scriptures!
I just rewrapped the ones
we gave him last year.

Hey! Those are for our home teachers!

Well, brothers and sisters, I can see that my time is just about up . . .

Read that part again about the "mighty change of heart."

I could get my home teaching done if the month had 32 days . . .

I was asked to speak on the dangers of apathy, but I didn't feel like it.

Ugh! Crickets again? I'm getting so sick of leftovers!

I don't know how the pioneers made it across the plains without duct tape.

Yes sirree! There's nothing like roughing it!

Grandpa, can't we read something besides Jonah and the whale?

No, we don't want to clean your room as a service project.

My lesson is on the gospel in its simplicity . . .

I guess I shouldn't have put the elephants, rhinos, and hippos all at the same end.

They're arguing about the meaning of the scripture, "Cease to contend one with another."

We're so blessed! New furniture *and* our year's supply of food!

The pioneers had it sooo easy. They only had to unload a handcart.

Is that what the scriptures mean? "As one crying from the dust . . ."

Did you remember to put out the curelom?

So, Nephi, I hear you came to pass . . .

It wasn't much of a date. I honked and honked, but she never came out.

He's right. There's nothing in the handbook about it.

We're playing Noah's ark.

Proposing? No, I'm just tying my shoe.

It's us, your home teachers. We know you're in there.

Sorry, I don't kiss on the last date.

No, I thought you brought the tickets . . .